A Gift For:

_____

From:

_____

Love is the whole
and more than all.

—e.e. cummings

One day
out of darkness
they shall meet,
and read life's meaning
in each other's eyes.

—Susan Mara Spalding

The moment

I heard my first love story

I started looking

for you.

—Shep Laughlin

If I had

never met you

I would have

dreamed you

into being.

—Natalia Bergmann

It is strange

that men will talk of miracles,

revelations, inspiration,

and the like,

as things past,

while love remains.

—Henry David Thoreau

In dreams

and in love,

there are no

impossibilities.

—Janos Arony

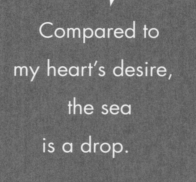

Compared to
my heart's desire,
the sea
is a drop.

—Adelia Prado

What is that you express

in your eyes?

It seems to me more than

all the words I have

read in my life.

—Walt Whitman

It would be a fine thing,

in which I hardly dare believe,

to pass our lives near

each other, hypnotized

by our dreams.

—Elie Smithsen

Could a greater miracle
take place than for us
to look through
each other's eyes
for an instant?

—Henry David Thoreau

I love you
not only for
what you are,
but for what I am
when I am
with you.

—Anthony Karaba

To love the one who loves you,

to admire one who admires you,

in a word, to be the idol

of one's idol, is exceeding

the limit of human joy;

it is stealing fire from heaven.

—Delphine de Girardin

Lovers don't
one day meet somewhere,
they're in each other
all along.

—Mitchell Prime

Whatever

      our souls

are made of,

      yours and mine

are the same.

—Emily Bronte

Within you,
I lose myself,
without you,
I find myself,
searching to be
lost again.

—Simone Cuellers

Give all to love.
Obey your heart.

—Ralph Waldo Emerson

Doubt that the stars are fire:

Doubt that the sun

doth move:

Doubt truth to be a liar:

But never doubt

that I love.

—William Shakespeare

Of all the

earthly music,

that which reaches

farthest into heaven

is the beating of a

truly loving heart.

—Henry Ward Beecher

Oh, how he loved her.

He gave her a look

you could have poured

on a waffle.

—Ring Lardner

She made my
blood stream feel
like the place that
the gods had to find
before they could
discover fire.

—Pat Conroy

I give thee what
could not be heard,
what has not
been given before:
The beat of
my heart I give.

—Edith M. Thomas

The loving are the daring.

—Bayard Taylor

We have both

lost ourselves,

but that is when

one reveals

most of one's self.

—Anais Nin

True love helps you
find things you didn't know
were missing in your life.
It helps you fill spaces
you didn't know
were empty.

—Kobi Yamada

It is only with the heart

that one can see rightly;

what is essential is

invisible to the eye.

—Antoine de Saint-Exupery

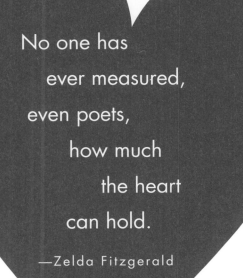

No one has
ever measured,
even poets,
how much
the heart
can hold.

—Zelda Fitzgerald

Love like ours can never die!

—Rudyard Kipling

What we have
once enjoyed we can
never lose.
All that we love deeply
becomes a
part of us.

—Helen Keller

We are

each of us angels

with only one wing.

And we can only fly

embracing each other.

—Luciano De Creschenzo

Then we sat
on the edge of the earth,
    with our feet dangling
over the side, and
    marveled that we
had found each other.

—Erick Dillard

Designed by Steve Potter
Compiled by Dan Zadra & Kobi Yamada

COM·PEN´·DI·UM™
Publishing

*E*nriching the lives of millions, one person at a time.™

This book may be ordered directly from the publisher, but please try your local bookstore first! To see Compendium's full line of inspiring products visit us at www.compendiuminc.com or call toll free 800-91-IDEAS.

ISBN: 1-932319-03-4

Printed in China